W9-BJE-472

STUDY GUIDE

NEXT LEVEL
THINKING

Also by Joel Osteen

ALL THINGS ARE WORKING
FOR YOUR GOOD
*Daily Readings from All
Things Work for Your Good*

BLESSED IN THE DARKNESS
Blessed in the Darkness Journal
Blessed in the Darkness Study Guide

BREAK OUT!
Break Out! Journal
Daily Readings from Break Out!

EVERY DAY A FRIDAY
Every Day a Friday Journal
*Daily Readings from
Every Day a Friday*

FRESH START
Fresh Start Study Guide

I DECLARE
*I Declare Personal
Application Guide*

NEXT LEVEL THINKING
Next Level Thinking Journal

THE POWER OF I AM
The Power of I Am Journal
The Power of I Am Study Guide
*Daily Readings from
The Power of I Am*

THINK BETTER, LIVE BETTER
*Think Better, Live Better
Journal*
*Think Better, Live Better
Study Guide*
*Daily Readings from Think Better,
Live Better*

WITH VICTORIA OSTEEN
Our Best Life Together
Wake Up to Hope Devotional

YOU CAN, YOU WILL
You Can, You Will Journal
*Daily Readings from You Can,
You Will*

YOUR BEST LIFE NOW
*Your Best Life Begins
Each Morning*
Your Best Life Now for Moms
*Your Best Life Now
Journal*
*Your Best Life Now
Study Guide*
*Daily Readings from
Your Best Life Now*
*Scriptures and Meditations
for Your Best Life Now*
Starting Your Best Life Now

STUDY GUIDE

NEXT LEVEL
THINKING

10 POWERFUL THOUGHTS
FOR A SUCCESSFUL
AND ABUNDANT LIFE

#1 *NEW YORK TIMES* BESTSELLING AUTHOR

JOEL OSTEEN

FaithWords

New York • Nashville

FaithWords
Hachette Book Group
1290 Avenue of the Americas
New York, NY 10104
faithwords.com
twitter.com/faithwords

First Edition: October 2018

FaithWords is a division of Hachette Book Group, Inc.
The FaithWords name and logo are trademarks of Hachette Book Group, Inc.

The publisher is not responsible for websites (or their content) that are not owned by the publisher.

The Hachette Speakers Bureau provides a wide range of authors for speaking events. To find out more, go to www.hachettespeakersbureau.com or call (866) 376-6591.

Literary development: Lance Wubbels Literary Services, Bloomington, Minnesota.

ISBN: 978-1-54602-652-5

Printed in the United States of America

10 9 8 7 6 5 4 3 2 1

Contents

Introduction

We are delighted that you have chosen to use this study guide that was written as a companion to *Next Level Thinking*. Too often we focus on our past, our mistakes, our failures, and the limitations of how we grew up and what people think of us. That keeps us stuck in bondage and defeat. But God created us to be free from all the shame, the guilt, the condemnation, the addictions, the feelings of never being good enough, and the carrying of pain of past hurts. It's interesting that before Jesus took His final breath on the cross, He declared, "It is finished." More than just declaring that His assignment on earth was finished, Jesus was stating in no uncertain terms that everything His assignment pertained to was finished—that He had provided us with everything we need to become everything He created us to be. It's done. Paid for. Finished!

This study guide is meant to help you see that everything you need to live a successful and abundant life has already been provided. All you have to do is believe it, receive it, and walk in it. The thoughts and questions addressed in the following pages will help you to train yourself to leave behind the negative mind-sets, the scarcity mentality, and the limitations others have put on you. It will help you learn to change your thinking and move forward into the next levels of the good things God has in store.

This study guide has been created so that it lends itself to self-study or personal development as well as small-group study or discussion, say in a care group or book club setting. Whichever the purpose you have in mind, you'll find great opportunity to personally be blessed as you take time to study and meditate on God's Word.

The format of each chapter is simple and user-friendly. For maximum benefit, it is best to first read the corresponding chapter from *Next Level Thinking*, and then work your way through the chapter in this study guide. The majority of the questions are personal, and taking the time to read through the chapters in the book and think through how each question can affect your life will give the study immediate personal application.

If you decide to use this study guide in a small group study, the most effective way is to go through each chapter on your own as preparation before each meeting. Take some time to read the relevant portions of text and to reflect on the questions and how they apply to you. This will give your group study depth and make the sessions more productive for all.

Because of the personal nature of this study guide, if you use it in a group setting or on a retreat, remember that confidentiality, courtesy, and mutual respect lay the foundation for a healthy group. A small group should be a safe place for all who participate. Don't let your conversations leave the small group. A small group is not a place to tell others what they should have done or said or think, and it's not a place to force opinions on others. Commit yourselves to listening in love to one another, to praying for and supporting one another, to being sensitive to their perspectives, and to showing each participant the grace you would like to receive from others.

CHAPTER ONE

Be a Barrier Breaker

So often we let our environment, how we were raised, and other people's expectations of us set the limits for our life. We adapt to what's around us. It's so easy to just fit in, to go with the crowd, to be like everyone else. But God didn't create you to be average. He created you to go beyond the norm and leave your mark on this generation. You have seeds of greatness on the inside. You're supposed to go further than the people who raised you. You're supposed to live better, be more successful, and set a new standard.

1. What was your immediate response to the statement "God created you to go beyond the norm and leave your mark on this generation"? Describe what you're thinking.

   ....

   ....

   ....

   ....

2. In what ways would you say you have let your environment and other people's expectations of you set the limits for your life? How have you adapted to it?

   ....

Don't let mediocrity become normal in your thinking.

   ....

   ....

   ....

   ....

   ....

Jesus speaks of how we are *in* the world, but we "are not *of* the world any more than [He is] *of* the world" (John 17:14).

3. You may be *in* a limited environment, but what does it mean that you don't have to be *of* it?

....

....

....

....

....

4. What limitations have other people tried to put on you? How did you respond?

....

....

....

....

....

5. What change in your thinking will help you take the limitations off yourself? Write a statement that declares you are finished with mediocrity.

....

....

....

....

....

Researchers put fleas in a container and then put a lid on the top. The fleas immediately tried to jump out, but they hit the lid again and again. Before long they realized they were stuck. Later when the researchers removed the lid, the fleas didn't try to jump out anymore. They had hit that lid so many times that they had become conditioned to thinking they couldn't get out. Even though the lid was off, they didn't even try.

6. Describe one example from your experience where you've tried and failed and become conditioned to thinking that you're stuck.

....

....

....

....

....

....

7. What valuable lesson can you take from the young man who grew up in the projects about your environment and limitations?

....

....

....

....

....

....

8. What truth about God will help you get rid of the thoughts that are holding you back?

....

*You are
not on
your own.*

....

....

....

....

....

9. What message did the school counselor give to the young man who got into trouble at school that broke down a stronghold in his thinking? Why was it so powerful?

     ....

     ....

     ....

     ....

     ....

     ....

     ....

     ....

     ....

10. Has anyone ever spoken truth like that into your life that broke a stronghold in your thinking? Or has a Scripture been used to break the power of thoughts that have held you back? Describe your experience and how God used that to change your life.

     ....

     ....

     ....

     ....

     ....

     ....

     ....

     ....

     ....

     ....

     ....

     ....

11. My father grew up very poor during the Great Depression. When he was seventeen years old, he gave his life to Christ as well as made a major decision that his children would never be raised in poverty. What lesson can you take from his example of becoming a barrier breaker?

....

....

....

....

....

....

12. Instead of just fitting into your environment, what change in your thinking and attitude will help you start seeing yourself as a barrier breaker, as the exception?

....

....

....

....

....

....

13. What can be the consequences of accepting and adapting to a limited environment?

....

....

....

....

....

14. As a teenager, my father felt seeds of greatness stirring inside. Have you felt a similar stirring inside your life? Describe it. What big dream do you have in your heart?

....

....

....

....

....

....

....

....

....

15. What message of hope do you feel God is personally speaking to your heart about fulfilling your dream and destiny? How can you start to apply this in your daily life?

....

....

....

....

....

....

....

....

....

Nothing will be sadder than to come to the end of life and realize what we could have become if we had just lived with an at-possibility mind-set instead of an at-risk mentality.

16. My father went back to his hometown and met some of his friends whom he hadn't seen in sixty years. What lesson can you take away from the contrast of their life experiences after having grown up in the same limiting environment?

....

....

....

....

....

....

....

....

You weren't created to get stuck, to settle and stay at the same place year after year. You were created to excel. There is potential in you right now just waiting to come out. You have gifts that will cause new doors to open, talent that will bring new opportunities.

17. Write an honest review of any excuses you are still holding on to that keep you in a place of low expectations. What steps of faith do you need to dare to take in order to break those barriers?

....

....

....

....

....

....

....

....

18. Glenn Cunningham went from being a boy who was told that he would never walk again to breaking the world record in the mile run in 1934. That required an amazing determination to overcome all the odds through a spirit of faith. What Scripture became his continual source of inspiration that he would not only walk but run?

....

....

....

....

....

....

....

....

You and God are a majority. You have what you need. You're a barrier breaker. You can defy the odds. You can beat the cancer, you can break the addiction, you can start the new business. You can go further than the experts have told you.

19. Search out and write down Scriptures that speak to your areas of need as Cunningham did. What is God saying to you that will recondition your mind?

> *Instead of dwelling on all the negative things people have said about you, dwell on what God says about you.*

....

....

....

....

....

....

....

....

20. What powerful principle was reflected in Roger Bannister's story that will help you start thinking better and believing that you are a can-do person?

....

....

....

....

21. When you break a barrier, what wonderful thing happens for those who come after you?

....

....

....

....

22. Hezekiah was raised in an environment of compromise, defeat, and mediocrity. But when he became king, what was the first thing he did? Describe why that is so important.

....

....

....

....

23. If Hezekiah were here today, what would he tell you about becoming a difference maker and becoming everything God created you to be?

....

....

....

....

CHAPTER TWO

You Are Fully Loaded

When God created you, He put in you everything you need to fulfill your destiny. He's intentional, down to the smallest detail, and when He laid out the plan for your life, He studied it carefully. He thought about what you would need, what it would take to get you there, then He matched you with your world. He gave you the talent you need, the creativity, the strength. You're the right size, and you have the right looks, the right personality, and the right family. You didn't get shortchanged. You are fully loaded and completely equipped for the race that's been designed for you.

1. How did you feel when you read the statement, "He put in you everything you need"? Write an honest review of how you see yourself in the light of that principle.

    ....

    ....

    ....

    ....

2. When God created you, He looked at you and said, "That was *very* good." He calls you "a masterpiece" (Eph. 2:10 NLT). Apply this powerful principle to how you see yourself. What difference does it make in practical terms?

    > *Next level thinking says you have the right looks, the right talent, and the right personality.*

    ....

    ....

    ....

    ....

    ....

3. If you had what somebody else has that you want, why would it be a burden rather than a blessing?

....

....

....

....

....

4. The Scripture says, "David had served God's purpose in his own generation" (Acts 13:36). How does this truth speak to the times when we feel we must be like someone else?

....

....

....

....

....

I've learned that it's easy to be me. I don't have to pretend. I don't have to perform. That takes all the pressure off. I can relax and just be myself.

5. Why is it so important to learn to be comfortable with who you are? In what ways have you found this to be true in your experience?

....

....

....

....

....

Nobody can beat you at being you. You can be a better you than anybody in the world.

Too often when we see someone who's more talented, more successful, more blessed, there's a tendency to be envious and think, *Why can't I do that? I want what they have.* If we're not careful, before long we'll be competing with them, trying to outperform them, outdress them, outdrive them, outwork them.

6. What is the problem when you start to compete with others? Who is the only one whom you should be competing with?

> *Instead of competing with people, celebrate them.*

....

....

....

....

7. King Saul lost the throne when he became jealous over David's popularity. What change in his perspective would have kept him from missing his destiny?

....

....

....

....

....

Someone has said, "Successful people are so focused on their own goals that they don't have time to look around to see what everybody else is doing."

8. Rather than be distracted and intimidated by others who have passed you by, what truth will you tell yourself to keep you focused on moving toward your purpose?

....

....

....

....

....

9. When you see someone who's blessed, who's rising higher, and you think, *Well, they've just had a lot of good breaks*, what do you need to realize about them, and about you, to keep you from getting sour about their success?

....

....

....

....

....

10. Describe a time in your life when you got into a competition with someone else and tried to keep up with them. What outcome did it lead to?

....

....

....

....

....

....

....

....

11. How can you keep from repeating that same painful mistake?

....

....

....

....

....

In the Scripture, John the Baptist was baptizing people and gaining a lot of attention. At one point the Jewish leaders came and asked him if he was the Christ. Without missing a beat John said, "I am not the Messiah."

12. Why is it important to know who you are not?

....

....

....

....

....

13. What do you need to understand about the sovereignty of God to have the right perspective on how He has made you?

....

....

....

....

....

....

....

14. Rather than compete with someone whom God has given more talents than you, or look down on someone who has less, what is the right perspective to take from now on?

> *Don't let outside pressures and other people squeeze you into becoming something that you're not.*

....

....

....

....

....

When I first started ministering, I had a lot of well-intentioned people giving me their opinions on how to lead the church, how to minister, what I should speak on. I felt the pressure to be who they wanted me to be. But I knew that most of their advice wasn't what God had put in my heart, and I had to be bold and say, "I am not that. This is who I am."

15. Who do you feel others think you are, and how have they put pressure on you to become what they think you should be?

_____

_____

_____

_____

_____

_____

_____

16. Who do you think you are, and who do you know that you are not? What is God showing you about the person He wants you to be?

_____

_____

_____

_____

_____

_____

_____

_____

You don't have to have a great gift for God to use you in a great way.

17. What gift promoted David to the throne? How did that gift become so effective?

....

....

....

....

....

18. Reflect upon why you should never discount your gift, no matter how small it seems.

....

....

....

....

....

....

19. There is something shut up in you, something big that's about to be released—dreams, businesses, ministries, gifts and talents that you haven't tapped into. What do you sense that God is doing in your life? What do you need to get ready for?

....

....

....

....

....

"His word is in my heart like a fire, a fire shut up in my bones" (Jer. 20:9).

20. When you face opposition that looks as though it's going to stop you from moving up to the next level, what key truth do you need to hold on to?

....

....

....

....

....

Sarah and Abraham were very old. She had been barren her whole life, but God said to Abraham, "I will bless her and will surely give you a son by her. I will bless her so that she will be the mother of nations; kings of peoples will come from her" (Gen. 17:16). Every circumstance said it was impossible. Yet God was saying, "Sarah, what I put in you is more than you can imagine."

21. God is saying the same thing to you: "There are kings in you. There is greatness in you. It's much bigger than what you think." What message of hope do you feel God is personally speaking to your heart about?

....

....

....

....

....

....

....

....

What God has put in you, He's still going to bring to pass. You're going to excel. You're going to be promoted. You are fully loaded. You don't see how it can happen, but get ready. What's been shut up in your spirit is being released!

CHAPTER THREE

The Odds Are for You

It's easy to go through life thinking of all the reasons why we can't be successful, why we won't get well, or why we'll never meet the right person. We look at our situations in the natural, such as an addiction or a financial difficulty, and think the odds are against us. But as long as you think the odds are against you, you will get stuck where you are.

1. The odds may be truly against you, and the circumstances may look impossible, but what can turn those around to be for you?

....

....

....

....

2. When you know the odds are for you, what ways do you see this impacting your life?

....

....

....

....

3. Why does God put you in situations where you can't see a way out?

....

....

....

....

4. Read the story of Gideon in Judges 7. Facing an overwhelming army of Midianites, why did God have Gideon reduce his army from thirty-two thousand to three hundred?

....

....

....

....

....

5. It looked like a setback for Gideon, but what was God doing for him?

....

....

....

....

....

6. Describe a situation in your past or present where the odds against you looked or look impossible. What is the right perspective to take when you feel like the underdog?

Next level thinking says the odds are for you.

....

....

....

....

....

....

....

....

....

....

7. What was it about Gideon that caused his enemies to be afraid? What is it about you that will cause you to defy the odds and go further than you ever dreamed?

....

....

....

....

....

God said, "And I will harden Pharaoh's heart, and he will pursue them. But I will gain glory for myself through Pharaoh and all his army, and the Egyptians will know that I am the LORD" (Exod. 14:4).

8. You may not like it that some people and circumstances have come against you; it's not fair, but why should you not complain? If you stay in faith, what will happen?

....

....

....

....

....

9. Read the story in Daniel 3 of the three Hebrew teenagers, Shadrach, Meshach, and Abednego, who wouldn't bow down to the king's golden idol. Why should you not panic when the furnace has been turned up seven times hotter in your life?

....

....

....

....

....

10. What valuable lesson can you take from the man who cut his hand and developed a severe infection? When you don't see a way—the financial situation looks too far gone, you've tried to break that addiction for years—why should you not let that cause you to think it wasn't meant to be?

> *Don't panic.*
> *Don't fall apart.*
> *It's a setup.*

11. Read the full story of the raising of Lazarus from the dead in John 11. If you were Mary or Martha, how do you think you would have felt toward Jesus when Lazarus died? What would you have said to Jesus when He finally arrived?

12. What remarkable lesson was Jesus demonstrating in waiting on purpose until the odds were against them?

The odds may be totally against you today, but God is totally for you. He has not brought you this far to leave you. Your circumstances may look dead. You've been asking and asking, but God didn't show up on time. Dare to trust Him. He has you in the palms of His hands. You may not see anything happening, but He is working behind the scenes, and when He speaks, dead things come back to life. He is not moved by the odds.

13. When the Compaq Center suddenly became available to us, it was like a resurrection, something better than I had ever dreamed. Describe a situation in your past when God brought back something to life that you thought was dead. Or describe a situation in the present where you're praying and believing for a resurrection.

....

....

....

....

....

....

....

14. What message from Lazarus's story do you feel God is speaking to your heart about?

....

....

....

....

....

....

....

15. Why was it not a coincidence that Jesus waited until the fourth day to heal Lazarus? What message does this tell you about how God is going to work in and through your life?

....

....

....

....

....

....

16. What encouragement and hope do you find in the example of the young lady who was one of twenty-six hundred applicants for only twelve scholarships?

....

....

....

....

....

....

17. Read the creation story in Genesis 1 and describe what the odds were of it happening.

> *God did not google it to see if it was possible.*

....

....

....

....

....

18. God spoke worlds into creation. What does that show that He can do for you?

....

....

....

....

....

....

19. Write a declaration of faith that you dare to believe Him to do that for you.

....

....

....

....

....

....

20. The odds looked overwhelming against Jimmy Wayne ever making something of his life, but God had a counselor named Cindy and an elderly couple in His plan to turn the odds for him. What assurance does this give you about His plan for your life?

....

....

....

....

....

....

As with Jimmy Wayne, the odds may be against you. You don't see any way your situation can work out. But God has the right people already lined up. The gifts He has put in you, the dreams, they didn't get canceled because you had bad breaks, because somebody did you wrong. They are still alive. You can still become who God created you to be. It may feel like the fire has been turned up seven times hotter, but don't worry. Your time is coming. God is saying, "The odds are for you."

21. Based upon what you have learned in this chapter, take a moment and reflect on how you can start living every day believing the odds are for you. Write a prayer to the Lord, telling Him how you feel as you reflect on these truths.

....

....

....

....

....

....

....

....

....

....

....

....

....

....

Like Jimmy, you're going to go further than you've ever dreamed, like the three Hebrew teenagers, you are going to come out of that fire without the smell of smoke, and like Lazarus, God is going to make you a living testimony. The odds are for you.

CHAPTER FOUR

Move Up to the Next Level

I t's easy to go through life weighed down by addictions, dysfunction, guilt, or the past and think that's who we are, but God created you to be free. When Jesus hung on the cross, before He took His final breath, He said, "It is finished." He wasn't just talking about the giving of His life for us and how He had finished His purpose. He was putting an end to all the negative things that could keep us from our destiny. He was saying, in effect, "The guilt is finished. The depression is finished. The low self-esteem is finished. The mediocrity is finished. It is all finished."

1. Read the account of Jesus' death in John 19 and the context for His declaration in verse 30, "It is finished," which means "paid in full." What was your immediate response to the statement that "It is finished" includes "putting an end to all the negative things that could keep us from our destiny"? Reflect upon your thoughts.

....

....

....

....

2. Are there things you're living with—guilt, feeling down on yourself because of past mistakes, not expecting anything good to come to you—to which you need to say, "It is finished"? Write down an example that you need to correct now.

....

....

....

....

....

3. You may have had bad breaks and gone through unfair situations, but God says He will pay you back double for the unfair things that have happened (see Isa. 61:7). What does that tell you about the person who did you wrong and hurt you?

> *No matter what someone did or didn't do to you, it does not change who you are.*

....

....

....

4. Read the story in John 5:1–15 of Jesus healing the man who had been disabled for thirty-eight years. Why did Jesus ask him, "Do you want to get well?" What do we need to realize about the dysfunctions and negative things we allow to stay in our lives?

....

....

....

....

....

5. Why do you need to be careful about whom you surround yourself with, especially in difficult times?

....

....

....

....

6. Name an area of your life that you need to change in order to surround yourself with the right people in order to "get well."

....

....

....

....

When Jesus asked the disabled man if he wanted to get well, instead of saying, "Yes, that's what I'm believing for," the man answered, "Sir, I don't have anybody to help me get in the water." He was justifying his condition. He was saying, "I'm this way because I'm at a disadvantage. Nobody will help me."

7. As long as you're making excuses for where you are—a bad childhood, an illness, being cheated by a business partner—you're going to get stuck. Take some time and list some of the excuses you have made or are making for where you are.

....

....

....

....

....

8. What truth about God will enable you to get rid of the excuses? Based on this truth, what can you tell the excuses?

....

....

....

....

....

Jesus said to the disabled man, "Get up! Pick up your bed and walk." Instantly the man was healed. He stood up, picked up his bed, and was able to walk out of there.

9. What is God saying to you about those negative things in your life that seem as though they're permanent, as though they are never going to change?

....

....

....

....

10. Faith played a major role in my father becoming a difference maker. How can faith empower you to do the same?

....

....

....

....

....

11. Describe a time when you felt well-meaning people in your life have tried to keep you in a limited environment.

....

....

....

....

You have to separate yourself from people who see you only for who you used to be and try to keep you in the same box that you grew up in. They'll try to put limitations on you and say, "You can't accomplish that dream. You're not that talented."

12. Read the story of the anointing of David to become the next king in 1 Samuel 16:1–13. Why do you think his father and brothers discounted him?

....

....

....

....

13. Have you ever felt discounted in a similar way? Describe your experience.

....

....

....

....

14. Even Jesus' own brothers did not believe in Him until after He rose from the dead. Reflect upon why you think they did not see Him as the Messiah.

....

....

....

....

....

15. How did Jesus' respond to His brothers' discounting of Him, and what does that tell you about how you should respond when you feel discounted?

....

....

....

....

....

My father could have stayed in that limited environment and accepted a life of poverty and lack, but he did what I'm asking you to do. He rose up and said, "It is finished. This may be where I am, but this is not who I am."

16. What can you learn from my father's experience that will help you take a step of faith that leads to a more blessed, abundant life?

> *One man didn't say, "I'm at a disadvantage. I've had bad breaks. This is as good as it gets."*

....

....

....

....

....

You can be the difference maker for your family. You can put an end to negative things that have been passed down. What you're dealing with may not have started with you, but it can stop with you.

17. What was your immediate response to the statement that you can be the difference maker for your family? In what way or ways does God want you to set a new standard for your family?

....

....

....

....

....

....

....

18. Describe how it's possible that you can take your family to a whole new level.

....

....

....

....

....

....

....

....

Now, do your part and have a new mind-set—an abundant mentality, a free mentality, a healthy mentality, a victorious mentality. Our family would not be where we are today if our father had kept a poverty mind-set, a scarcity mentality, thinking, *I'm at a disadvantage. I've had bad breaks.*

It's time to announce to anything that's holding you back, "It is finished. This is a new day. I'm drawing the line in the sand. As for me and my house, we will serve the Lord. We will live free from addictions. We will be generous and help others. We will accomplish our dreams and become everything we were created to be."

19. My friend's father gave him a very difficult lesson that showed him that they could reach a higher standard. What does that tell you about where you have started in life? Using his father's statement of faith, write your own statement of faith that you will start a generational blessing for you and your family.

> *"Son, I brought you here to show you that though this is where we come from, this is not who we are."*

....

....

....

....

....

....

Abraham was living in a limited environment. God told him to leave his country, to leave his extended family behind, and go to a land that He would show him. God was saying, "Abraham, you have to leave what's familiar, leave what you grew up with."

20. Have you ever felt God was telling you to leave behind the negative mind-sets you were raised with? Describe your experience.

....

....

....

....

....

....

The prophet Isaiah says, "Enlarge the place of your tent, and let them stretch out the curtains of your dwellings; do not spare; lengthen your cords, and strengthen your stakes" (Isa. 54:2 NKJV). Make room for God to do a new thing.

21. What is God saying to you about making room for Him to increase you? Be specific on what you can do to keep a limited environment from holding you back.

....

....

....

....

....

22. What does it mean to you that God is a progressive God? Why is it so important to hold to this truth?

....

....

....

....

....

23. Read the story in 2 Samuel 12 of David and his newborn baby. Write an honest review of how you think you would have responded if you had been David.

....

....

....

....

....

We all have things in life that we don't understand. It's easy to live negatively. But if we're going to receive the double portion God has promised for the unfair things that have happened, we have to do as David did and say to the past, say to the things you don't understand, "It is finished. I'm not going to dwell on what didn't work out. I'm not going to try to figure out why. I'm going to let it go and keep moving up to the next level."

24. After reading this chapter, what have you discovered that you need to say "It is finished" to and get ready for the new things God is about to do?

....

....

....

....

....

....

....

25. Write a prayer to the Lord, telling Him how you feel as you reflect on these truths.

....

....

....

....

....

....

....

This is a new day. Things that have held you back are being broken right now. You're going to step into a new level of freedom. You're going to break generational curses and start generational blessings. You're about to see beauty for ashes, healing, promotion, and breakthroughs. It's headed your way!

CHAPTER FIVE

Recognize Your Value

Too often we base our value on how someone is treating us, how successful we are, how perfect a life we've lived. The problem is that all those things can change. If you're trying to get your value from people, then if they hurt or disappoint you, you're going to feel devalued. If you base your value upon your achievements—how much money you make or the title behind your name—then if something happens and you don't have that position or your business goes down, your sense of value will go down. Some people don't feel good about themselves because they've made mistakes. Now they're living with insecurities, feeling inferior. They base their value on their performance.

1. Your value should be based solely on the fact that you are a child of the Most High God. Reflect on this truth and write out some specific ways that applies to your own sense of value.

> *Value is not based on what you do, what your income is, or who you know.*

....

....

....

....

....

2. You have royalty in your blood, but the enemy works overtime trying to devalue you. Have you recognized that is true in your life? In what ways?

....

....

....

....

....

....

3. Nothing you ever do, nothing you ever achieve, and nothing you ever overcome will make you any more valuable. How do you feel knowing this? Write a statement of faith that declares you are who God says you are.

....

....

....

....

....

4. Read Luke 4:1–13. When the enemy tempted Jesus to turn a stone into bread, what was he trying to do? What was Jesus' response?

....

....

....

....

....

5. When the enemy offered Jesus all the kingdoms in the world if He would worship him, what was he trying to do? What was Jesus' response?

....

....

....

....

....

6. When the enemy tempted Jesus to jump off the top of the temple and demonstrate how the angels would protect Him, what was he trying to do? What was Jesus' response?

....

....

....

The enemy tried to deceive Jesus into proving Who He was. Many people live in a proving mode. They can't feel good about themselves unless they prove to people that they are
important, prove to their coworkers that they are talented, and prove to their critics that
they really are okay. There is a constant struggle going on in their lives.

7.   We all struggle with proving ourselves. What areas of your life are you facing now that
     involve trying to prove yourself?

     ....

     ....

     ....

     ....

     ....

     ....

     ....

     ....

8.   What valuable lessons can you take from Jesus' example in Luke 4 that will help keep
     your faith strong when the enemy tries to deceive you into proving who you are?

> *You don't
> have to prove
> anything to
> anyone.*

     ....

     ....

     ....

     ....

     ....

     ....

     ....

     ....

9. Today there's so much emphasis on name brands. How can that become a problem for us personally? Has it been a problem for you? How so?

....

....

....

....

....

10. Why is your name more important than any name brand?

....

....

....

....

....

11. Why is living with possession-based values so exhausting?

....

....

....

....

....

12. What truth will keep you from living frustrated about needing popularity, possessions, or performance to feel good about yourself?

....

....

....

....

....

When Jesus was riding into Jerusalem to celebrate the Passover, a large crowd celebrated His arrival, shouting, "Hosanna! Blessed is he who comes in the name of the Lord!" (John 12:13). But a few days later, those same people were shouting, "Crucify Him!" (John 19:6). When Jesus went to trial and needed His closest friends to support Him, most of His disciples fled. When He asked them to stay up and pray, they fell asleep.

13. Describe a time in your life when you based your value on people's support, how much they approved you, and then they stopped doing that. How did it impact you?

....

....

....

....

....

....

....

....

14. As you look back on that experience, what did you learn from it? Did your response to it help you deal with future similar experiences?

....

....

....

....

....

....

....

....

If you don't know who you are without other people, then if they leave, you'll be lost. They'll take you with them, because your identity was caught up in who they made you to be. Then you'll have to try to find somebody else to tell you who you are.

15. Describe one example from your experience where you felt lost in this way and its effect upon you.

....

....

....

....

....

....

....

....

16. Based upon who God says you are, write down words of truth to help keep you from living frustrated by messages that come to you telling you just the opposite.

Don't give away your power. Don't put your identity, your value, into somebody else's hands.

....

....

....

....

....

....

....

....

Even good people who love you can't give you everything you need. Sometimes we're putting pressure on people to keep us feeling approved, validated, and secure, but they can't. You have to go to your heavenly Father. Let them off the hook. They're not your Savior. You already have a Savior. He's on the throne. Go to Him and not to people.

17. Why can other people never keep us fixed and feeling validated?

....

....

....

....

You may feel as though you never received the approval from your parents or your family. Even now, they don't celebrate you. They don't affirm you. But the truth is, it's not about you. It's about their own issues, their own insecurities. Don't spend your life trying to get something from them that they cannot give.

18. Reread 1 Samuel 16. What would have happened if David had to have his family's approval to become who he became?

....

....

....

....

19. Have you felt you have your family's approval? How has your response to that impacted the person you have become and are still becoming?

....

....

....

....

Quit trying to make people be for you who are never going to be for you. Quit feeling inferior because somebody close to you is not celebrating you. If you're not getting it, that means you don't need it to become who you were created to be. Yes, it may be hurtful, but it is not going to keep you from your destiny.

20. When David was discounted by his own family, where did he turn? Write out Psalm 27:10 and take some time and memorize this powerful verse of Scripture.

....

....

....

....

....

21. When a group of watches all look basically the same, what can give one watch so much more value than the others?

....

....

....

....

....

22. Apply this principle to your perspective of your own intrinsic value. Be specific.

....

....

....

....

> *Sometimes we don't realize who we are.*

....

....

If you're going to recognize your value, you have to see yourself as amazing, as wonderful. It's not because of who you are, but because of Who made you. Life will try to make you feel as though you're anything but amazing. Disappointments, betrayals, and rejection will try to steal your sense of value. But all through the day, you need to remind yourself, "I am amazing. I am a masterpiece. I have been wonderfully made." Don't go around feeling ordinary, when in fact you're extraordinary. Don't discount what God has created.

23. After reading this chapter, what did you discover about the person God made you to be? Write a prayer to the Lord, telling Him how you feel as you reflect on these truths.

_____

_____

_____

_____

_____

_____

_____

_____

_____

_____

_____

_____

_____

_____

_____

_____

The Scripture says you belong to God. You don't have to prove anything. You don't have to try to impress people. Just be who you are. Be amazing.

CHAPTER SIX

Live with the Boldness of a Son

Because of negative things we've gone through in the past—disappointments and unfair situations—or even mistakes we've made, it's easy to forget who we really are. Too often we've developed a slave mentality. We think we're at a disadvantage, so we don't pursue our dreams or believe for good breaks to come our way. We live as though we're a slave to an addiction, a slave to depression, a slave to mediocrity, a slave to others' approval.

1. It is never easy to admit we have a slave mentality in areas of our lives, but as long as we allow it to remain, it will limit our life. Take some time and reflect on what those areas have been in your life.

....

....

....

....

....

2. While we may struggle against a slave mentality, what is the truth about who we really are? In what ways have you recognized that as true in your life, and in what ways have you not?

....

....

....

....

> *"Dear friends, now we are the children of God"* (1 John 3:2).

....

....

....

After the Israelites had been in slavery in Egypt for four hundred years, God sent plagues on the Pharaoh and his people until he finally let them go. When the Israelites headed out toward the Promised Land, they were excited that their dream of freedom had finally come true…until Pharaoh changed his mind and came chasing after them, quickly approaching with his army as the Israelites came to a dead end at the Red Sea.

3. Describe the debate that must have been playing back and forth in the minds of the Israelites as Pharaoh and his chariots closed in behind them.

....

....

....

....

....

4. Describe the same debate that is taking place about you. What is the good news about how the debate can be brought to an end?

....

....

....

....

5. How do you, as a child of God, not only think differently but talk differently from a slave? Write out some specific ways that you need to start thinking and speaking differently.

....

....

....

....

....

Pharaoh came chasing after the Israelites. In other words, the past came chasing after them, reminding them of all the negative things they had been through. The past will always come chasing after you. The mistakes you've made, the disappointments, the failures, and the hurts are saying, "You're not a son. Look what you've been through. It wasn't fair. You prayed, and it didn't work out."

6. Name some of the troublesome ways that your past is still chasing you today.

....

....

....

....

....

7. What truth about God will keep you from being a slave to your past?

....

....

....

....

8. Just as Pharaoh thought he owned the Israelites, your past will tell you that it owns you. Write a declaration of freedom that you tell the enemy whenever he brings up the past.

....

....

....

....

....

Nothing that's happened in your past and nothing that you've done have to keep you from the good things God has in store. Don't be a slave to your past.

9. God not only freed the Israelites from slavery, but He eliminated their oppressor so they wouldn't have to live with the threat that they might be taken back to slavery. God has not only freed us from sin, from guilt, from depression, and from sicknesses, but what has He done to our enemy? Do you see yourself as free that way?

> *"Behold, I have given you authority to tread on...all the power of the enemy"* (Luke 10:19 ESV).

10. What negative report did the ten spies bring to Moses, and what does that tell you about how they still saw themselves?

11. If you have struggled in an area for a long time, what change in your thinking will help you break the bondages that have held you back? Apply this powerful principle to the negative things that look permanent in your life. Be specific.

Although it was good that God freed that first group of two million from slavery, that wasn't God's best. Those people never made it into the Promised Land because they still saw themselves as slaves. But God didn't give up on them. He didn't say, "I'm done with this family." Forty years later, God took their children into the Promised Land, because that next generation had a different mind-set.

12. Read God's promise in Deuteronomy 6:10–12 of what He was about to give to the people of Israel when they entered the Promised Land. Name those specific provisions. What is its message of hope for you today and for the future?

_____

_____

_____

_____

_____

_____

Now, don't talk yourself out of it. "That's not me. I've reached my limits. My family always struggles." Get rid of that slave mentality and start having an abundant mentality.

13. Take a moment and reflect on whether you have an abundant mentality. What changes in your thinking will help you start living a more abundant life every day?

> *"I have come that they may have life, and that they may have it more abundantly"* (John 10:10 NKJV).

_____

_____

_____

_____

_____

_____

14. Describe the difference in attitude between a service repairman coming into a home and a son or daughter coming into the home. What is the basis for this difference?

....

....

....

....

....

15. Write out Hebrews 4:16. Take some time and memorize this powerful truth. How can you start to apply this in your life today in a way that pleases God?

....

....

....

....

....

....

Jesus says, "It is your Father's good pleasure to give you the kingdom" (Luke 12:32 NKJV).

16. Are you trying to earn God's goodness, thinking that then maybe you'll deserve God's blessings? How do Jesus' words tear down a slave mentality?

....

....

....

....

....

....

17. Read the parable of the prodigal in Luke 15:11–32 and retell it as though you were the son. How do you think your father would respond if you returned home? How would you feel when you see your father standing at the end of the driveway waiting for you?

....

....

....

....

....

....

....

....

18. Describe a time in your life when you got off course and believed a lie that God wouldn't have anything to do with you. What outcome did it lead to? How can you keep from repeating that same painful mistake?

....

....

....

....

....

....

....

When you gave your life to Christ, you were born into the family of God. You can't get unborn. You can't make a mistake that's too big. You can't get too far off course. You may disqualify yourself, but God never disqualifies you.

"The father said to his servants, 'Quick! Bring the best robe and put it on him. Put a ring on his finger and sandals on his feet. Bring the fattened calf and kill it. Let's have a feast and celebrate. For this son of mine was dead and is alive again; he was lost and is found.' So they began to celebrate" (Luke 15:22–24).

19. What is God showing you about Himself through the example of the prodigal's father? What message of hope do you feel God is personally speaking to your heart?

....

....

....

....

....

....

....

....

20. Where do you need to get in agreement with God and start believing that He loves You as His son or daughter in this way? Write a bold prayer to the Lord, telling Him how you feel about His love.

You can start a party up in heaven right now!

....

....

....

....

....

....

....

21. Write out some specific situations or areas of your life where you need to change from a cheese-and-crackers mentality to a son's abundant mentality. How will you start to step up to the table?

....

....

....

....

....

22. Read Judges 8:18. Although Gideon felt inadequate to do what God was calling him to do, how did his enemies see him? What valuable lesson can you take from Gideon when you feel at a disadvantage?

....

....

....

....

....

....

23. Using the "I see"s at the end of this chapter as your base, write out your own confession of who you are as a child of the living God.

....

....

....

....

....

....

CHAPTER SEVEN

Know You Are Loved

After Victoria and I had been dating for about nine months, a friend told me that Victoria had said she thought she loved me. My friend was so excited, but I had a problem with two words—*she thinks*. That could mean she does love me, or it could mean she doesn't. She's still trying to figure it out. It could go either way. *She thinks* didn't give me any confidence at all. In fact, it made me think, *I need to do more and try to really impress her, or I might not be good enough. She thinks* put me under more pressure. Eventually, Victoria went from "I think" to "I know," and that was over thirty-one years ago.

1. When you *know* that somebody loves you, what difference does it make?

....

....

....

....

....

2. Why do a lot of people live with an "I *think* God loves me" mentality? Have you struggled with the thought that God loves you conditionally? Describe examples from your past experiences.

> *God never changes His mind about you.*

....

....

....

....

....

Sometimes we're trying to clean ourselves up, trying hard to be good enough, and then we'll believe that God really loves us. But there's nothing you can do to make God love you any more or any less. It's a gift. Just receive it by faith.

3. Write out Romans 8:38–39 and listen to hear the Lord whispering these words to you. Take some time and memorize these powerful verses of Scripture.

....

....

....

....

4. Psalm 139:8–10 says, "If I go up to the heavens, you are there; if I make my bed in the depths, you are there. If…I settle on the far side of the sea, even there…your right hand will hold me fast." What does that tell you about God's love for you?

....

....

....

....

....

5. The apostle John says, "See what great love the Father has lavished on us, that we should be called children of God!" (1 John 3:1). Describe what the unconditional love of God means.

....

....

....

....

....

There was a popular self-improvement book that was adapted into a movie called *He's Just Not That Into You*. It was about guys not really liking a girl and how the girl shouldn't waste her time. Can I tell you that God is just the opposite. He's way into you. If He's taking the time to number your hairs, to know your thoughts, to plan out all your days, do you really think there's anything you can do to cause Him to stop loving you?

6. What are you learning about God's love for you? Write a prayer to the Lord, telling Him how you feel as you reflect on this truth.

> *When you go from "I think" to "I know," you'll quit trying to earn God's love.*

7. Rather than refer to himself by name in his Gospel, the apostle John referred to himself as "the disciple whom Jesus loved" (John 13:23). When Matthew, Mark, and Luke wrote their Gospels, they referred to themselves by using their own names. What do you think they would have thought of John's describing himself this way?

8. What was John showing when he stated that he knew God loved him? How do you feel, knowing that you can do the same?

_____

_____

_____

_____

_____

9. Read John 11:3. When Lazarus was very sick and close to death, on what basis did Mary and Martha ask their good friend Jesus to come and pray for Lazarus?

_____

_____

_____

_____

_____

Sometimes, we're trying to convince God that we love Him. "God, I went to church last week. God, I've been performing so well. Would You please help me now?"

10. What is it that moves God? What pleases God? What is God showing you about how He wants you to come to Him? How can you align your thoughts closer to His?

_____

_____

_____

_____

_____

11. If your child came to you embarrassed and ashamed, head down, begging you to help, how would that make you feel when you love them with all your heart? How do think God feels when we come to Him asking for help with that same attitude?

12. What gave Alexandra the confidence to know that she would receive a yes to her request before she even asked?

13. Think for a moment about the difference it could make in your life today if you felt the same way about our heavenly Father. Write out some specific ways.

14. What powerful principle was reflected in Alexandra's assurance that Victoria would not miss the mother-daughter weekend even though Victoria already had commitments?

....

....

....

....

....

....

15. How does that reflect on how God thinks and feels about you, His child?

....

....

....

....

....

> *"And so we know and rely on the love God has for us. God is love"* (1 John 4:16).

We are all God's favorite. You are the one whom He loves. Nothing you can do will make God love you more. You might as well believe that you are His favorite right now. He may not be pleased with all your behavior, but that doesn't change His love for you.

16. Write a prayer of thanks to the Lord, telling Him how you feel as you reflect on being His favorite.

....

....

....

....

....

....

Read the story of a tax collector named Zacchaeus in Luke 19:1–10. He was despised and hated by everyone in his community as dishonest and a cheat. Yet Jesus picked him out of a huge crowd of people and said He wanted to come to his house for dinner.

17. What do you imagine that Zacchaeus felt in that life-changing moment of time?

....

....

....

....

The name *Zacchaeus* means "pure one." I doubt if anyone in that crowd ever called him Zacchaeus. They probably called him "fraud," "crook," "cheater," or "scum."

18. When Jesus purposefully said, "Zacchaeus, pure one, come down," what does that tell you about how God sees people different than we do?

....

....

....

....

....

19. What valuable lesson can you take from the fact that Jesus chose Zacchaeus over all the other "good" people that day?

....

....

....

....

First John 4:10 says, "This is real love—not that we loved God, but that he loved us and sent his Son as a sacrifice to take away our sins" (NLT).

20. What does this tell you is the problem when you try to perform to gain God's love?

....

....

....

....

....

21. Read the story in John 8:1–11 about the lady who was caught in the act of adultery. When her accusers had left, what did Jesus not say to her, and what did He say to her? Be careful to note why the order of His response is so important.

....

....

....

....

....

....

22. How is the real love that she felt so different from what religion sometimes tells us?

....

....

....

....

....

....

....

When my brother was little, my parents would put him in his bed at night, and then they would go and get in their own bed. Their rooms were just a few feet apart, down a short hallway. My father would always say, "Good night, Paul," and Paul would answer back, "Good night, Daddy. Good night, Mother." One night, after they had said their good-nights, Paul was a little afraid and said, "Daddy, are you still in there?" My father said, "Yes, Paul, I'm still here." A few seconds later, Paul asked, "Daddy, is your face turned toward me?" My father said, "Yes, Paul, my face is turned toward you." Somehow, it made Paul feel better just knowing that our father's face was turned toward him.

23. What message of hope do you feel God is personally speaking to your heart through Paul's story? How do you feel, knowing that your heavenly Father's face is always turned toward you?

> *Real love is not about your love for God; it's recognizing the great love God has for you.*

CHAPTER EIGHT

Approve Yourself

Too many people go around feeling as though something is wrong on the inside. They don't really like who they are. They focus on their faults and weaknesses. They're constantly critical toward themselves. There's a recording of everything they've done wrong that is always playing in their mind. They wonder why they're unhappy and don't realize it's because they have a war going on inside.

1. You're not supposed to go through life feeling wrong about yourself. What is the key to dealing with the feeling that you will never measure up?

> *"We all, with unveiled face...are being transformed into the same image from glory to glory"* *(2 Cor. 3:18 NKJV).*

2. What is the problem with not liking yourself?

Keep your flaws in perspective. Every person has something they're dealing with. You may see someone who looks as though they have it all together. They're happy, enjoying their life, but you need to realize they're on the Potter's wheel.

3. The prophet Isaiah says, "O Lord, you are our Father. We are the clay and you are the Potter. We are all formed by your hand" (Isa. 64:8 TLB). Why is it so important to understand this principle?

    ....

    ....

    ....

    ....

    ....

4. What would happen to the man who struggled with his temper as long as he stayed down upon himself?

    ....

    ....

    ....

    ....

5. What areas of your life are you facing that you find easy to stay negative toward yourself because you can't get them right? Instead of beating yourself up, what attitude do you need to take that will allow God to work?

    ....

    ....

    ....

    ....

    ....

6. The Scripture says in Hebrews 12:2, "[Looking away from all that will distract us and] focusing our eyes on Jesus, who is the Author and Perfecter of faith" (AMP). Apply this powerful principle to whatever you consider your flaws and weaknesses.

7. This doesn't mean you don't try to improve. What does it mean?

8. There are plenty of areas in which we need and want to improve, but what perspective do we need to maintain while we're in the process of change?

Our lives are a work in progress. God has His own timetable. While He's changing us, we need to feel good about who we are and enjoy our life, knowing that God will get us to where we're supposed to be. It's very powerful when you can say, "I like who I am. I feel good about myself. I'm proud of who God made me to be."

9. Most people cannot say that about themselves. What do they usually say instead?

....

....

....

....

....

10. If you're going to live in victory, when the accuser reminds you of some area in which you're not up to par, what do you have to say in response?

....

....

....

....

....

11. When you take this stand, what do you need to expect that the enemy will tell you? How must you be prepared to answer?

....

....

....

....

....

Think about the apostle Paul. He said, "I want to do what is good, but I don't. I don't want to do what is wrong, but I do it anyway" (Rom. 7:19 NLT). Even he wasn't perfect. He still struggled in some areas.

12. If Paul had lived down on himself, thinking, *Why can't I get it right?* what wouldn't he have done, and what wouldn't we have today?

....

....

....

....

....

....

13. If Paul could accomplish all that he did with his flaws and weaknesses, what assurance and encouragement does this give you that you can accomplish your dreams?

....

....

....

....

....

....

14. For change to come in your life, why is it so important to stay on the Potter's wheel?

....

....

....

....

....

....

15. God says, "Before I formed you in the womb I knew you [and approved of you as My chosen instrument]" (Jer. 1:5 AMP). What does this say about your weaknesses and shortcomings?

....

....

....

....

....

....

16. Write out some specific ways that you need to start approving yourself.

> *It's time to start feeling good about who you are.*

....

....

....

....

....

....

17. The apostle Paul says that we are to put on "the breastplate of God's approval" (Eph. 6:14 TLB). It's not going to happen automatically. Write a statement of faith that declares you are putting on God's approval. Make a point to declare your statement boldly each morning.

....

....

....

....

....

....

Many people live with the heaviness, that feeling that there's something wrong with them, because they're not putting on the breastplate of God's approval. It's a breastplate, meaning that it covers the most important area of your life, which is your heart. You may have many areas in which you still struggle, but living condemned, feeling as though you're unworthy and don't deserve God's blessing, is going to cause you to get stuck.

18. Thoughts will come saying that you can't feel good about yourself. All through the day in your thoughts what do you need to be saying?

....

....

....

....

....

....

....

19. After Jesus was baptized in the Jordan River by John the Baptist, a voice boomed out of the heavens saying, "This is My beloved Son, in whom I am well pleased" (Matt. 3:17 NKJV). Up to this point in Jesus' life, He hadn't performed one miracle. What does that tell you about God's approval of you?

....

....

....

....

....

....

....

....

The most important relationship you have is your relationship with yourself. If you don't get along with yourself, you won't be able to get along with anybody else. It will affect every relationship, including your relationship with God. If you're living under guilt, feeling condemned and unworthy, you won't go to God with boldness. You won't ask Him for your dreams.

20. Jesus says, "Love your neighbor as yourself" (Matt. 22:39). Why can't you love your neighbor if you don't first love yourself?

_____

_____

_____

_____

_____

_____

_____

The Scripture says our faith is made effective when we acknowledge everything good. If you're acknowledging everything you don't like about yourself—your flaws, your shortcomings, your failures—your faith is not going to be effective.

21. Rather than taking inventory of everything you don't like, write an honest inventory of what is right with you.

_____

_____

_____

_____

_____

_____

Some people have never once said, "I like myself. I like my gifts. I like my personality. I like my looks. I'm happy with who God made me to be." You may say, "Well, I'm not going to say I like myself. That's weird." But if you don't like yourself in a healthy way, other people are not going to like you. You project what you believe on the inside. If you feel wrong about yourself, you will project inferiority and unfriendliness to others.

22. Using the declaration above, write your own statement declaring that you love yourself and are happy with the way God made you.

....

....

....

....

....

....

....

....

23. After reading this chapter, what are you discovering about yourself? Write a prayer to the Lord, telling Him how you feel as you reflect on these truths.

....

....

....

....

....

....

....

When you love yourself, chains of guilt, low self-esteem, and inferiority are broken in the unseen realm. Don't you dare go through life being against yourself.

Get the Contaminants Out

I don't know about you, but I've found bitterness is always knocking at the door—people do you wrong, you didn't get the promotion, you came down with an illness. You can't stop difficult things from happening to you, but you can choose how you respond to them. If you hold on to the hurt and dwell on the offense, you open the door to bitterness. When you're bitter, it affects every area of your life. Bitterness poisons your attitude to the point where you see everything in a negative light.

1. We all have known people who became bitter. How would you describe them in general terms?

....

....

....

....

....

2. Have you ever felt bitter about something difficult that's happened to you? Describe your experience and how it affected your relationships, your joy, and your dreams.

> *When you're bitter, you can't enjoy life. There's always something wrong.*

....

....

....

....

....

....

Some people remain bitter over something that happened long ago. They're bitter because they were mistreated or because a relationship didn't work out. You have to let it go.

3. What change in your thinking will help you let go of bitterness?

....

....

....

....

....

4. What happens when you hold on to bitterness?

....

....

....

....

....

5. Reflect on a time in your life when what started as a small offense that was done to you, not a big deal, grew into a big problem. Describe why it happened.

....

....

....

....

....

....

....

The Scripture says, "See to it that…no 'root of bitterness' springs up and causes trouble, and by it many become defiled" (Heb. 12:15 ESV). Notice that bitterness is described as a root. You can't see a root; it's hidden, it's underground. But here's the problem. A bitter root produces bitter fruit. If you have a root of bitterness, it will contaminate your life.

6. How does the young man who felt he'd been treated unfairly by his employer demonstrate the effects of allowing a root of bitterness to spring up?

....

....

....

....

7. Proverbs 4:23 says, "Guard your heart with all vigilance…for out of it flow the springs of life" (AMPC). What does that mean, particularly as you consider a root of bitterness?

Quit letting what's on the outside get on the inside of your heart.

....

....

....

....

....

8. When the apostle Paul said, "Alexander the metalworker did me a great deal of harm. The Lord will repay him for what he has done" (2 Tim. 4:14), how does that reflect a mature attitude? What was Paul saying about the offense and the offender?

....

....

....

....

While we can't see a tree's roots, the roots are where the tree gets its life. When your roots are healthy, positive, and hopeful, that's feeding you with life, strength, encouragement, and hope. But if you have bitter roots, you're not being fed the right nutrients. You wonder why you lack energy, why you don't laugh much, why you don't dream like you used to—it's because the bitter roots are feeding you bitterness, self-pity, and anger. That's draining all the life, the strength, the passion, and the joy out of you.

9. Psalm 139:23 says, "Search me, God, and know my heart." Spend some time and ask Him to show you if there is anything that is causing you to be bitter. What is He showing you that needs to be uprooted and gotten rid of?

....

....

....

....

....

....

....

....

10. You can't get rid of a bitter root on your own. Write a prayer to the Lord, asking Him to help you to do whatever needs to be done to release the bitterness and restore your joy.

....

....

....

....

....

....

....

Years ago there was a severe outbreak of disease in a small village in Africa. When experts were sent to test the water from the mountain stream where the village got its water from, they discovered the crystal clear water was contaminated. The researchers traveled upstream for many days to the source of the stream, which looked fine on the surface. But divers found that pigs had somehow fallen in and drowned right at the source and became wedged at the opening. Now, all the water was being contaminated as it flowed past the dead pigs. Once they removed the pigs, the water was perfectly fine.

11. Apply this same principle to the power of forgiveness in your life. Be specific as to the reasons why forgiving others is so important in keeping contaminants out.

....

....

....

....

....

....

....

12. In addition to the prayer you wrote on question 10, write a bold statement of faith that you are moving forward with God as your vindicator and living healthy, whole, and secure.

....

....

....

....

....

....

....

Read Ruth 1. A lady name Naomi had some tough times. She was a widow who had lost her husband and then, years later, both of her married sons also died. Sometimes life doesn't seem fair. She had grown bitter and given up on her dreams.

13. You can have more than your share of bad breaks, as did Naomi, but what truth about God will keep you from growing bitter?

....

....

....

....

....

....

Naomi was so discouraged she didn't think she could go on. She even changed her name from Naomi, which means "my joy," to Mara, which means "bitter." She said, "Call me Mara, because the Almighty has made my life very bitter. I went away full, but the LORD has brought me back empty" (Ruth 1:20–21).

14. Have you ever gone out full, with big dreams and big goals, but things didn't work out the way you had planned? Describe your experience and how you responded.

> *Just because you've been through loss doesn't mean you're not going to win again.*

....

....

....

....

....

....

What's interesting is that even though Naomi changed her name, the Scripture never refers to her as Mara. It keeps calling her Naomi.

15. You may have changed your name, so to speak, to Mara, but God didn't change your name. What does He call you? What name do you need to get back to?

....

....

....

....

....

....

....

Instead of sitting around feeling bitter, Naomi started helping her widowed daughter-in-law Ruth. She turned her focus away from her own problems and started helping somebody else. When she did, her joy began to come back. She never dreamed she could be that happy again, but this once bitter woman was now more fulfilled than ever.

16. When you're tempted to be bitter, one of the best things you can do is to get your mind off yourself and go be a blessing to others. What valuable lesson can you take from Naomi's example and apply to specific areas of your life?

....

....

....

....

....

....

....

In Mark 16, Jesus had been crucified and His body was laid in a tomb. When Mary Magdalene and two other women went to the tomb early the next morning, they found the stone had been rolled away. They went into the tomb and saw an angel, which frightened them. He said to them, "You're looking for Jesus, but He is not here. He has risen! He is going ahead of you into Galilee. There you will see Him." Notice that the angel said, "He is not *here*. He is *there*." The angel was saying, in effect, "I know this looks bad. I know you're disappointed, but don't stay *here*. Something better is waiting for you *there*."

17. "Here" is the disappointment, the bad medical report, the dream that didn't work out. Sometimes God doesn't comfort us in the "here." Why not?

> *God is not in your past, in what didn't work out. He's in your future.*

18. What would have happened if the three ladies had stayed at the tomb in self-pity?

19. Are you living in the "here," while God is waiting for you "there"? What is the good news that can help take you from the "here" to the "there"?

20. In chapter six we considered the parable of the prodigal (Luke 15:11–32). What was the attitude of the older brother when his father celebrated the return of the prodigal with a fatted calf and music and dancing?

....

....

....

....

....

21. With or without the older brother joining in, the celebration went on. What does that tell you about holding on to bitterness and unforgiveness?

....

....

....

....

....

22. Today is a gift. Life is fragile. Time is too short to live offended and bitter, in self-pity. After studying this chapter, what truths will you take with you to help you live free from bitterness in the future?

....

....

....

....

....

....

CHAPTER TEN

Remove the Shame

Starting in our childhoods, we've all heard the phrase "Shame on you." When you didn't clean your room, you were told, "Shame on you." When you were mean to your little brother or sister, once again it was, "Shame on you." As adults, the words still play in our thoughts. If you fell back into a bad habit, you told yourself, "Shame on you." If you went through a divorce, the message was repeated over and over, "Shame on you." We don't realize how destructive shame is. We use it to try to convince people to do better, but shame does just the opposite. It causes us to feel guilty and unworthy.

1. There was a voice that was constantly whispering to the young lady who put her baby up for adoption, "Shame on you." Shame is one of the enemy's favorite tools. He is called "the accuser of our brethren, who accused them before our God day and night" (Rev. 12:10 NKJV). Write out some specific ways that shame has been used against you.

> The enemy will remind you of every mistake and every failure you've ever made, even about things that weren't your fault.

The Scripture speaks of how God has removed our shame. Whether it was your fault or somebody else's fault, you don't have to carry the heavy load of guilt, or beat yourself up over past mistakes, or feel wrong on the inside.

2. When the enemy says, "Shame on you," what does God say?

....

....

....

....

....

3. Our refusal to accept shame doesn't excuse us from taking responsibility for our actions when we've done wrong to someone. How should we always treat someone whom we've wronged?

....

....

....

....

....

4. The question is not whether God will forgive you but whether you will forgive yourself. Why does the enemy work overtime to keep you under guilt and shame? What amazing step even beyond forgiving you does God take (see Isa. 43:25)?

....

....

....

....

....

During the hundreds of years when the Israelites were slaves in Egypt, they were very beaten down, not only physically but emotionally. They were constantly told that they were no good, that they couldn't do anything right, that they would never measure up, and that they deserved to be punished.

5. Over time, what did this mistreatment and abuse do to the Israelites' sense of value?

....

....

....

....

6. As the Israelites were approaching the Promised Land, God said to them, "Today I have rolled away the reproach of Egypt from you" (Josh. 5:9). What did He mean by that, and why did that need to happen before they went into the Promised Land?

....

....

....

....

....

7. In the same way, before you can reach your highest potential, you have to get rid of any shame. What is your Egypt, so to speak, and what is God saying to you about it?

....

....

....

....

....

> *Now it's up to you to accept what God has done.*

I know a man who was happily married, but he let his guard down and got involved with another woman. It happened one time, and that was it. He knew it was wrong and felt so badly about it. He asked God to forgive him, but year after year went by and he carried a sense of shame and guilt, as though he had to settle for second best.

8. Why did this man continue to feel a heaviness of guilt? What had the enemy been telling him all those years?

....

....

....

....

9. The apostle Paul says, "The weapons we fight with…have divine power to demolish strongholds" (2 Cor. 10:4). What did the minister say to this man that tore down the stronghold of guilt and shame in this man's life?

....

....

....

....

10. Maybe like this man, you know God has forgiven you, but you still have a sense of unworthiness as though you don't deserve it. Where do you need to get in agreement with God and start believing this is true for you?

....

....

....

....

....

Don't let negative events from your past become your identity. Don't let a failure, a divorce, a bankruptcy, or an addiction become who you are. It's easy to take all the blame and let it consume you with guilt. Before long you become known as the man who blew his marriage, or the woman who was abused, or the young person who has the addiction.

11. How is your identity different from what you have done? Why is it so important to remind yourself of who you are when thoughts of guilt and shame try to label you?

....

....

....

....

....

In the Scripture, names were given a lot more meaning and significance than they do today. Isaac had a son whom he named Jacob. *Jacob* means "a supplanter, one who is a trickster, a swindler, a deceiver." Every time someone said, "Hello, Jacob!" they were saying, "Hello, trickster!" "Good morning, Jacob. Good morning, con man."

12. After hearing this year after year, what did Jacob become?

....

....

....

13. Have you found this principle to be true in your life? How so?

....

....

....

....

....

Genesis 32 records that later in Jacob's life, he got tired of living as a deceiver and decided to return with his family to his parents' home. One night on the journey back, he went down to the brook to get alone with God, where an angel appeared to him in the form of a man. The angel asked Jacob what his name was, and he responded, "I am Jacob." He was saying, "I am a cheater. I am a deceiver. I am dishonest." The angel didn't say, "You're right, Jacob, and you should be ashamed of yourself."

14. What remarkable words did the angel say to Jacob? Rather than shaming Jacob, how did the angel's pronouncement change Jacob's life?

....

....

....

....

....

....

....

15. Maybe like Jacob, you are wearing negative labels today. Have you allowed your circumstances, your failures, or even other people put a label on you that says "not valuable, not worthy, addicted, bad parent, blew his marriage, doesn't deserve to be blessed"? What is God saying about whether we deserve to be blessed? What is He changing our names to today?

> *This is what grace is all about.*

....

....

....

....

....

....

If you're still struggling with a bad habit, an addiction, or a wrong attitude, there is no shame in asking for help. Sometimes we think we're supposed to be perfect, so we can't let anybody know we aren't. Don't let shame keep you isolated. Real healing begins when we get honest. The Scripture says, "Admit your faults to one another and pray for each other so that you may be healed" (James 5:16 TLB).

16. Everyone has issues. Why is it important to have someone stand with you in faith on some issues? What type of person should you look for to help? Do you have that person?

....

....

....

17. Even in the Scripture, all the heroes of faith had their weaknesses. What do you see in some of their lives that gives you encouragement in your daily walk?

....

....

....

Many times the things you're struggling with didn't start with you. They were passed down. Now this is your opportunity to put an end to it. You can be the one to break the negative cycle in your family. The first step is to shake off the shame. Don't be embarrassed. Don't try to hide it. You don't have to go through life pretending.

18. What is the key to overcoming anything that is holding you back? Write down 1 John 4:4 and begin to commit it to memory.

....

....

....

....

19. What powerful principle was reflected in the teenage girl who struggled with anorexia that will help you to confront any issues of shame?

....

....

....

....

....

Some people live with a sense of shame because of something that happened to them that wasn't even their fault. You may have been mistreated or somebody took advantage of you. The enemy will twist things and try to convince you that it was your fault. Don't believe those lies. If they did you wrong, the problem was with them, not you.

20. God says, "You will forget the shame of your youth and remember no more the reproach" (Isa. 54:4). What does that mean?

> *God saw every person who lifted a finger against you, every tear, and every hurt.*

....

....

....

....

....

21. Why must you forgive the people who did you wrong and let it go? What old labels do you need to take off, and what new labels do you need to put on?

....

....

....

....

....

22. God says, "Instead of your [former] shame you shall have a twofold recompense; instead of dishonor and reproach [your people]…shall possess double [what they had forfeited]" (Isa. 61:7 AMPC). What does this promise state that He will do for you?

....

....

....

....

....

23. What truth created the "explosion on the inside" of the lady who grew up wearing the labels "Illegitimate" and "Not up to par"? What did she begin to tell herself to reprogram her thinking?

....

....

....

....

....

24. Do you desire to be set free from every trace of guilt, shame, and heaviness? This is your day to be set free! How can you start to reprogram your thinking and live a shame-free life today?

....

....

....

....

....

....